Copyright © 2017 Dea Bernadette D. Suselo
All rights reserved.

ISBN: 9781793060662

www.facebook.com/DeaBernadette
Instagram: dea_bernadette

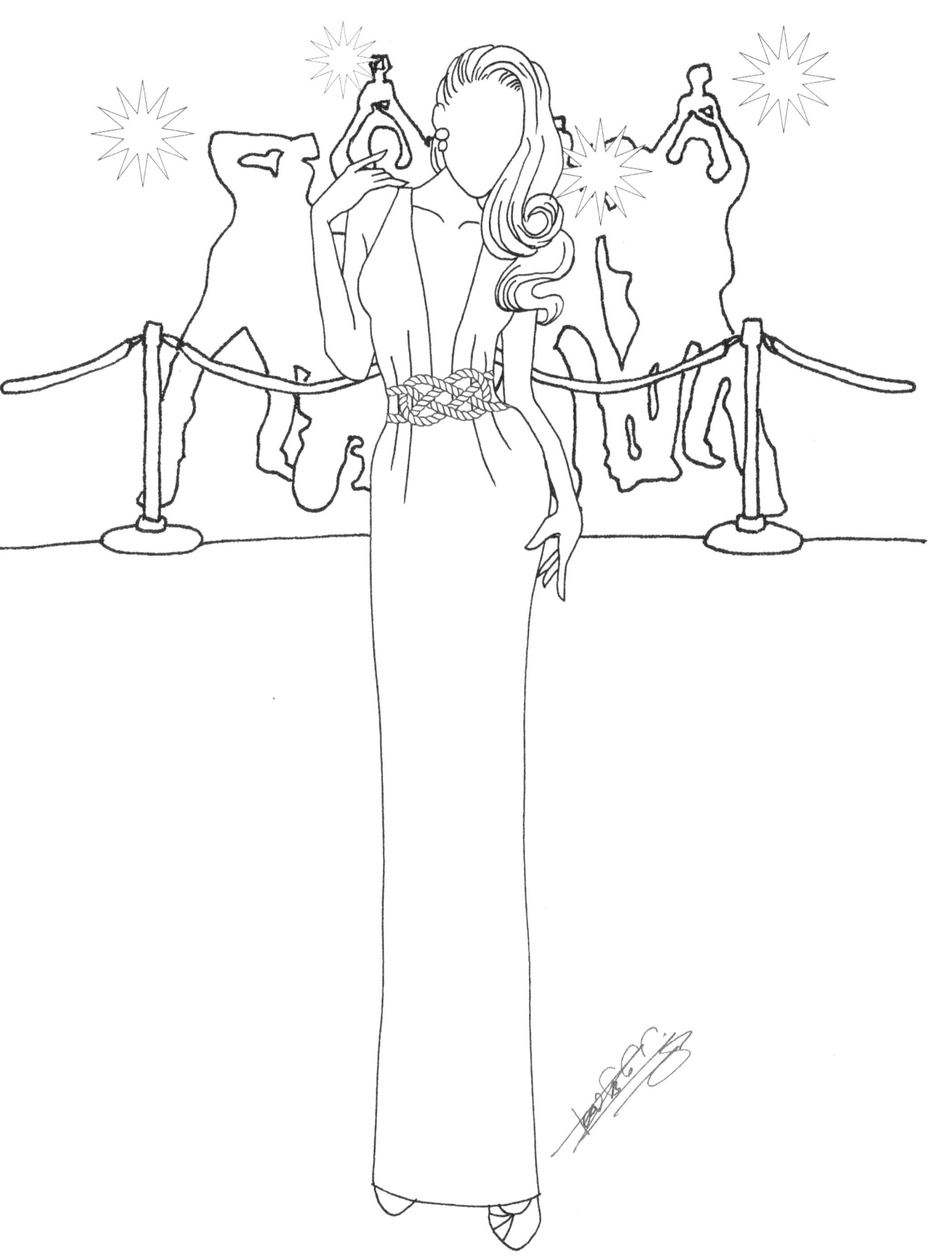

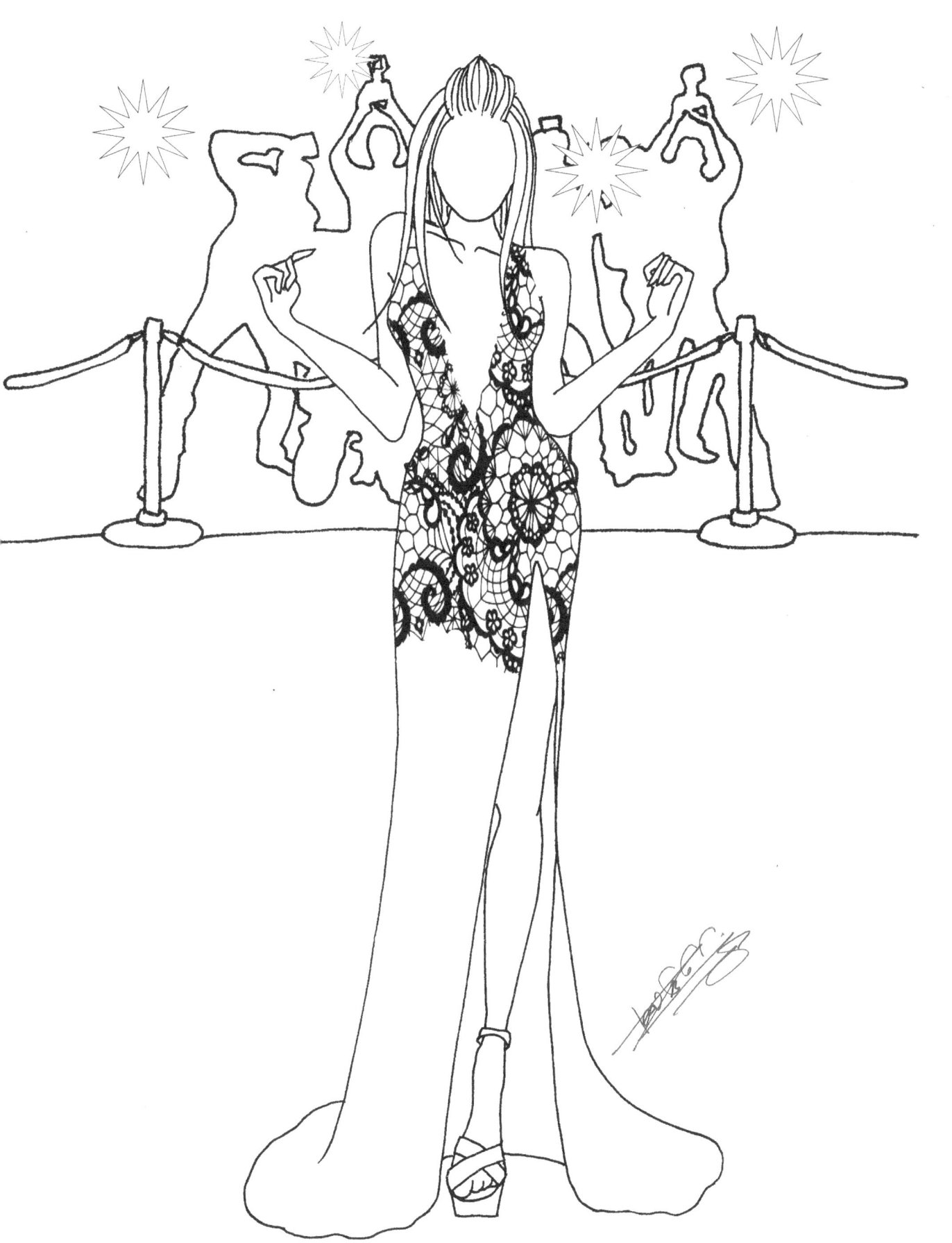

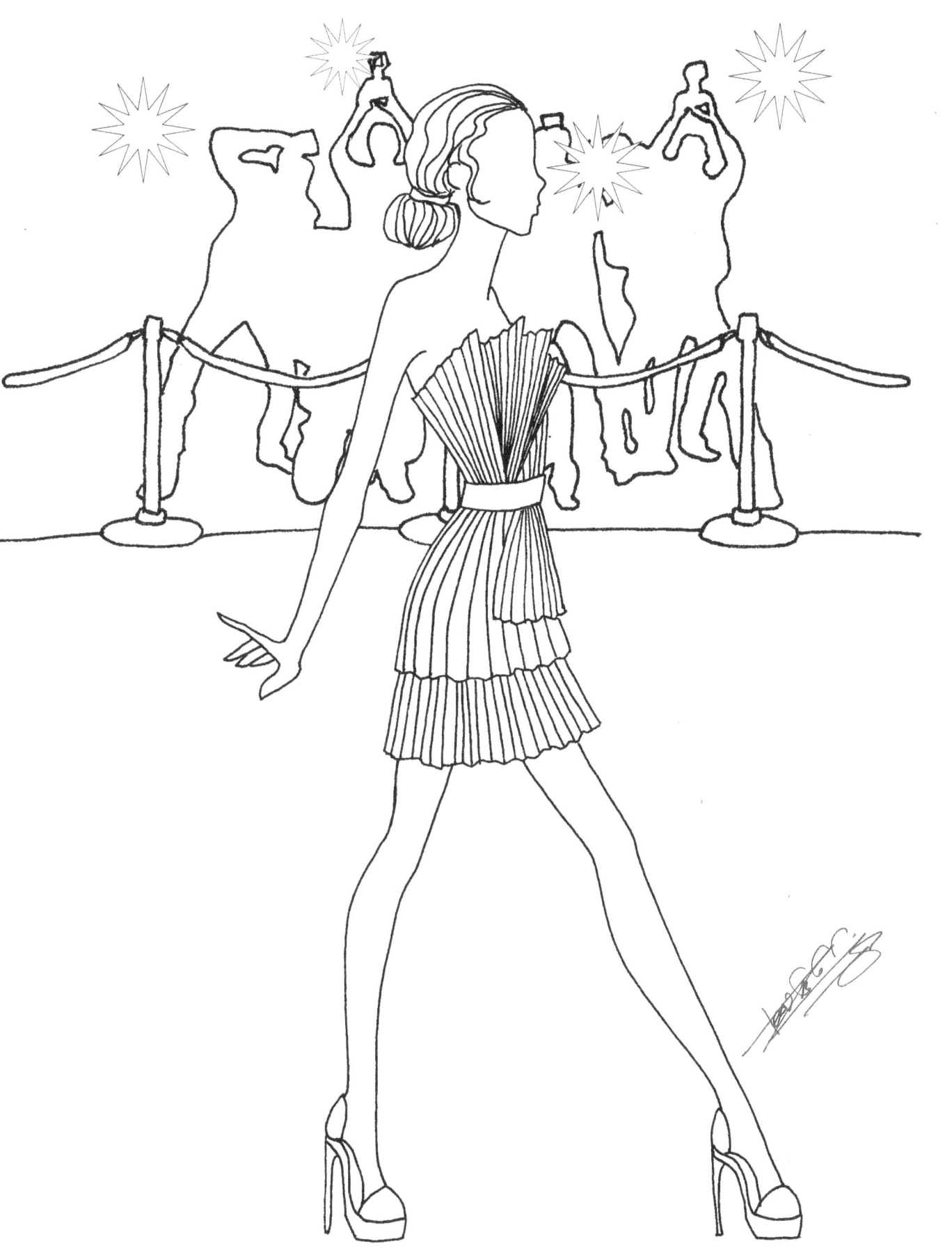

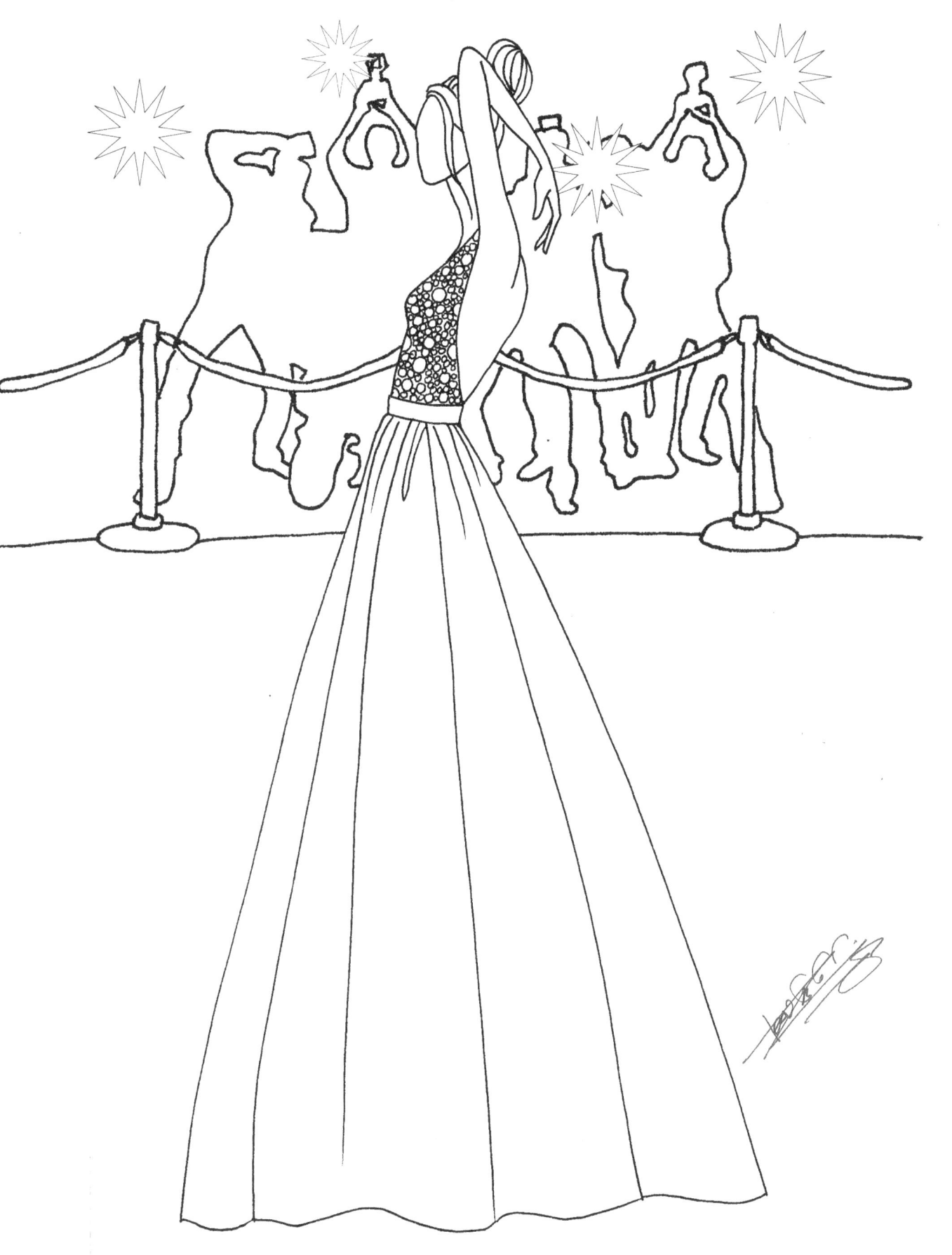

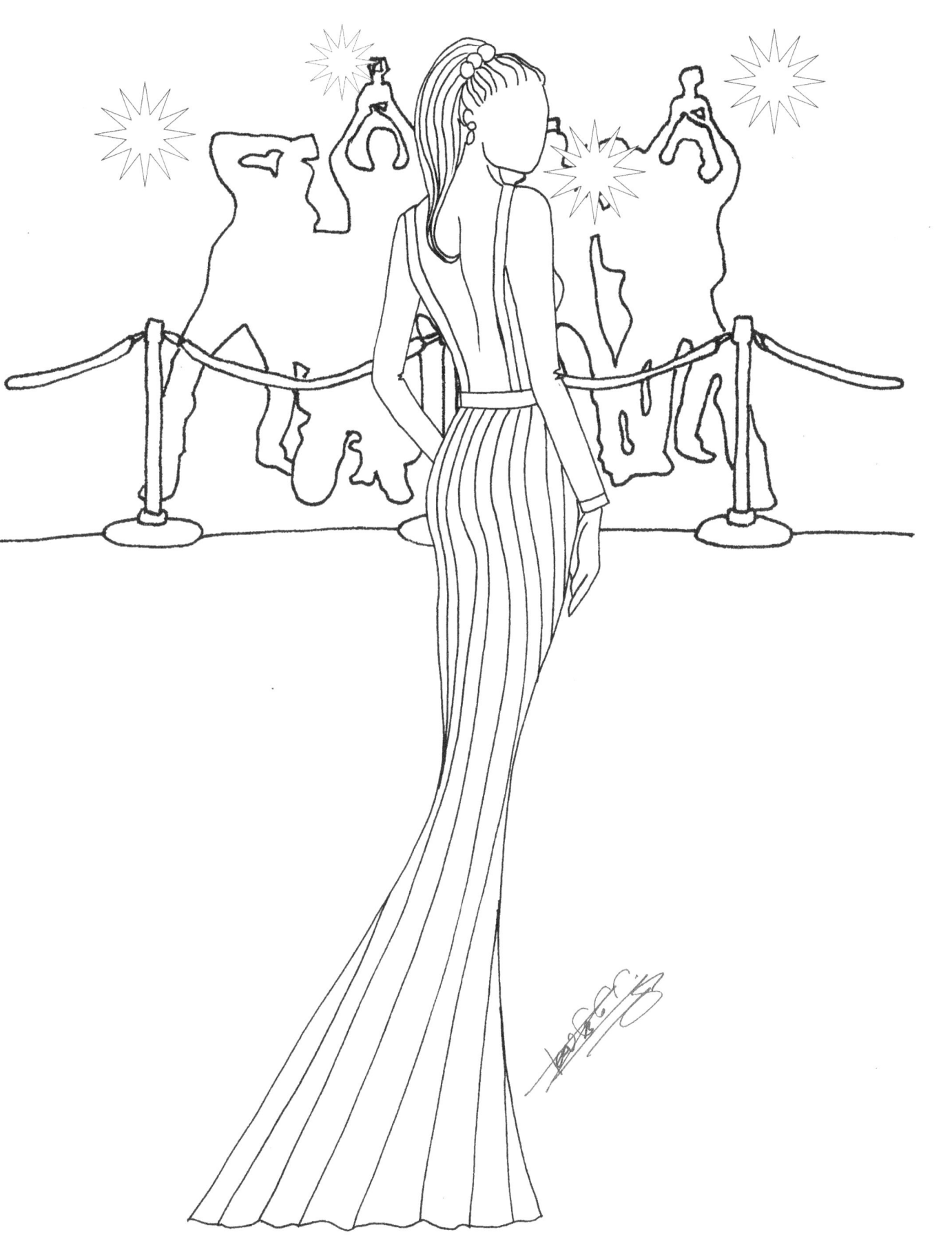

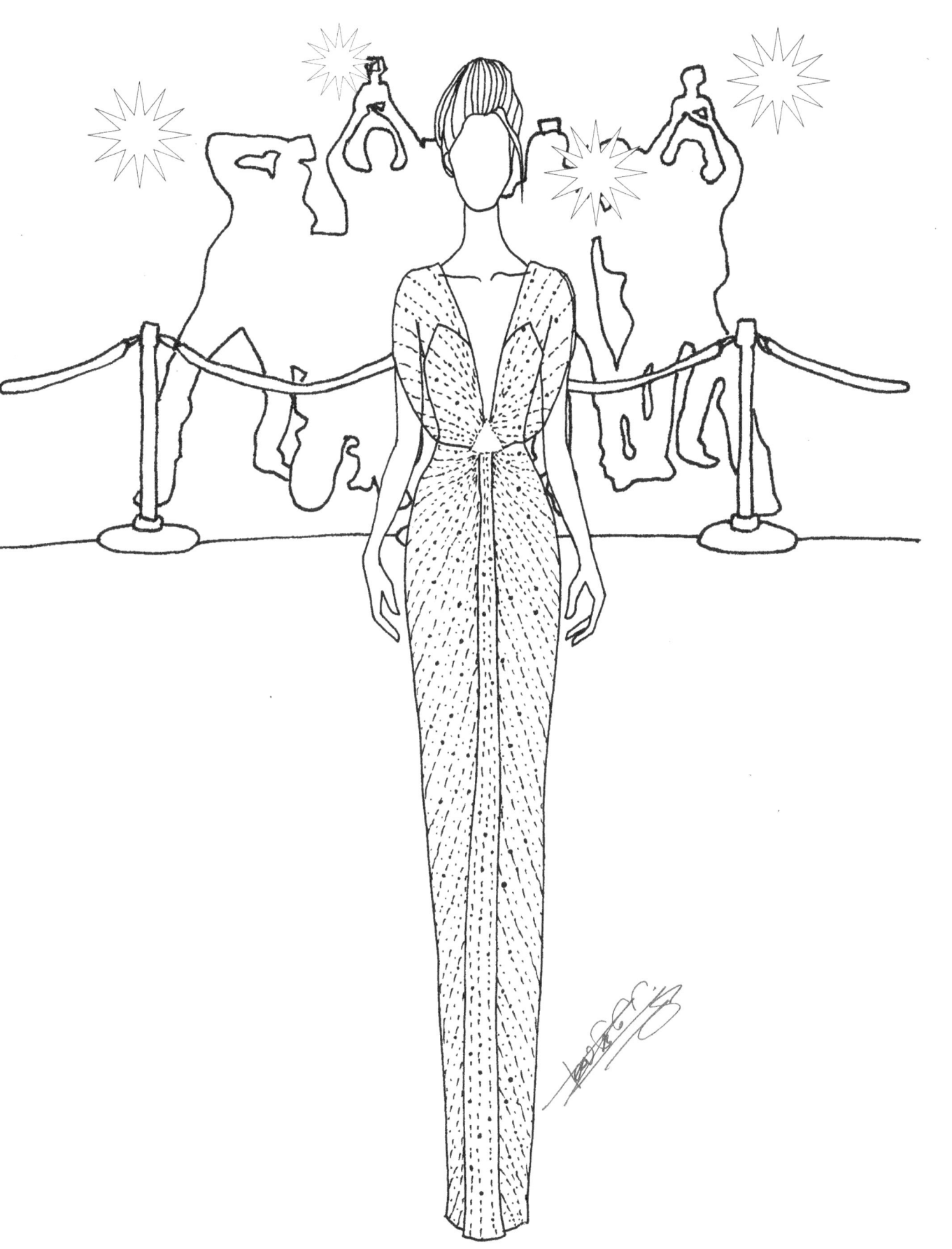

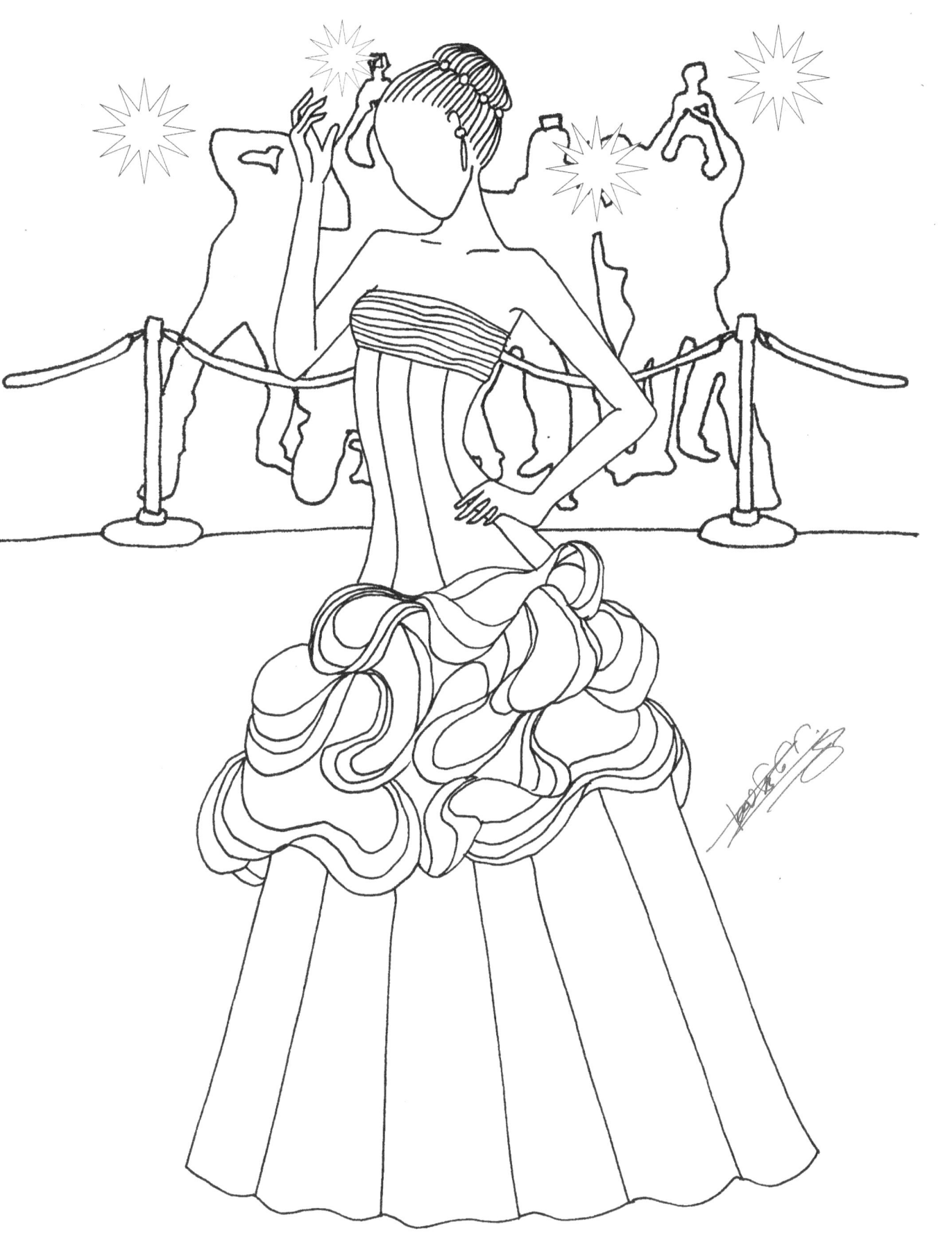

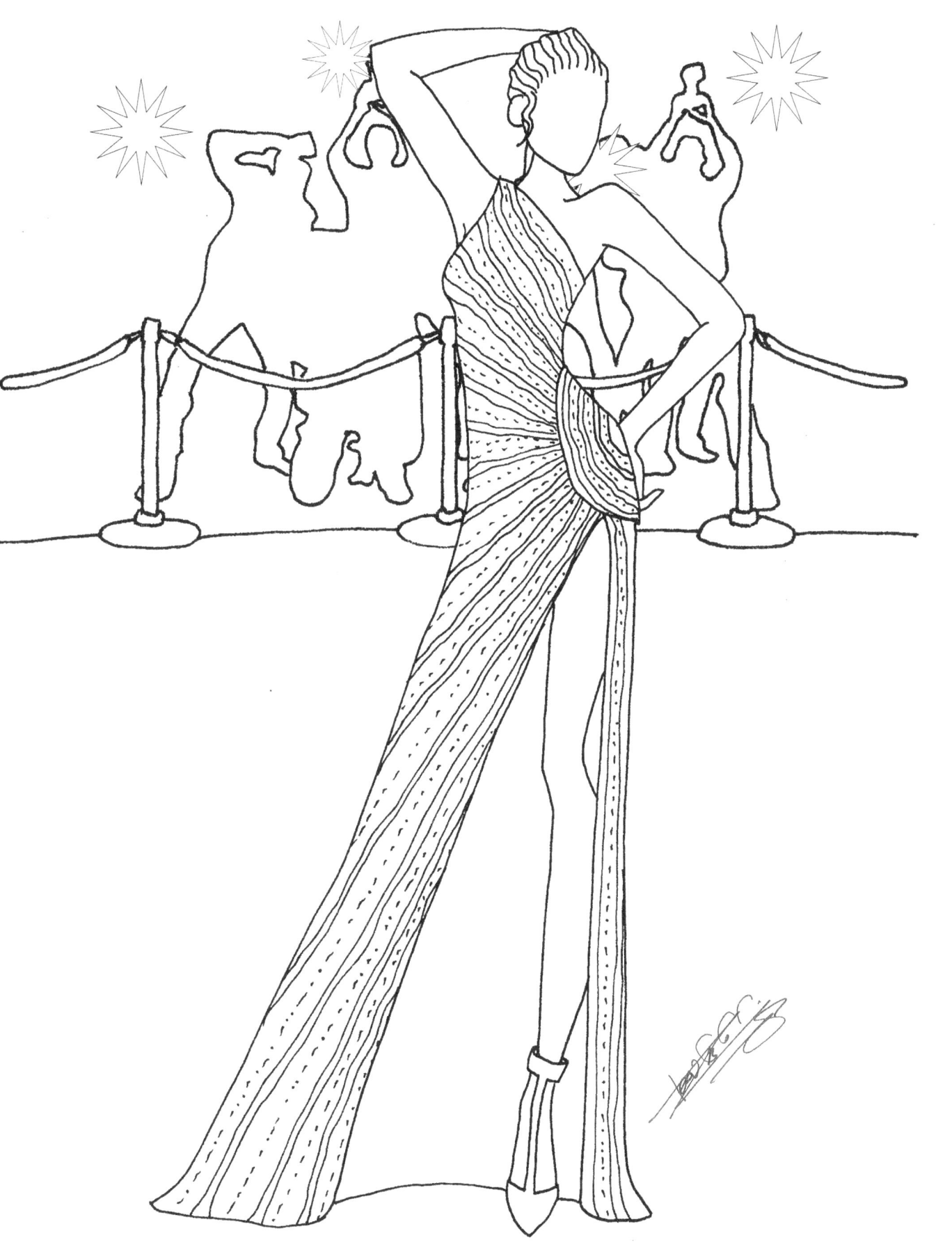

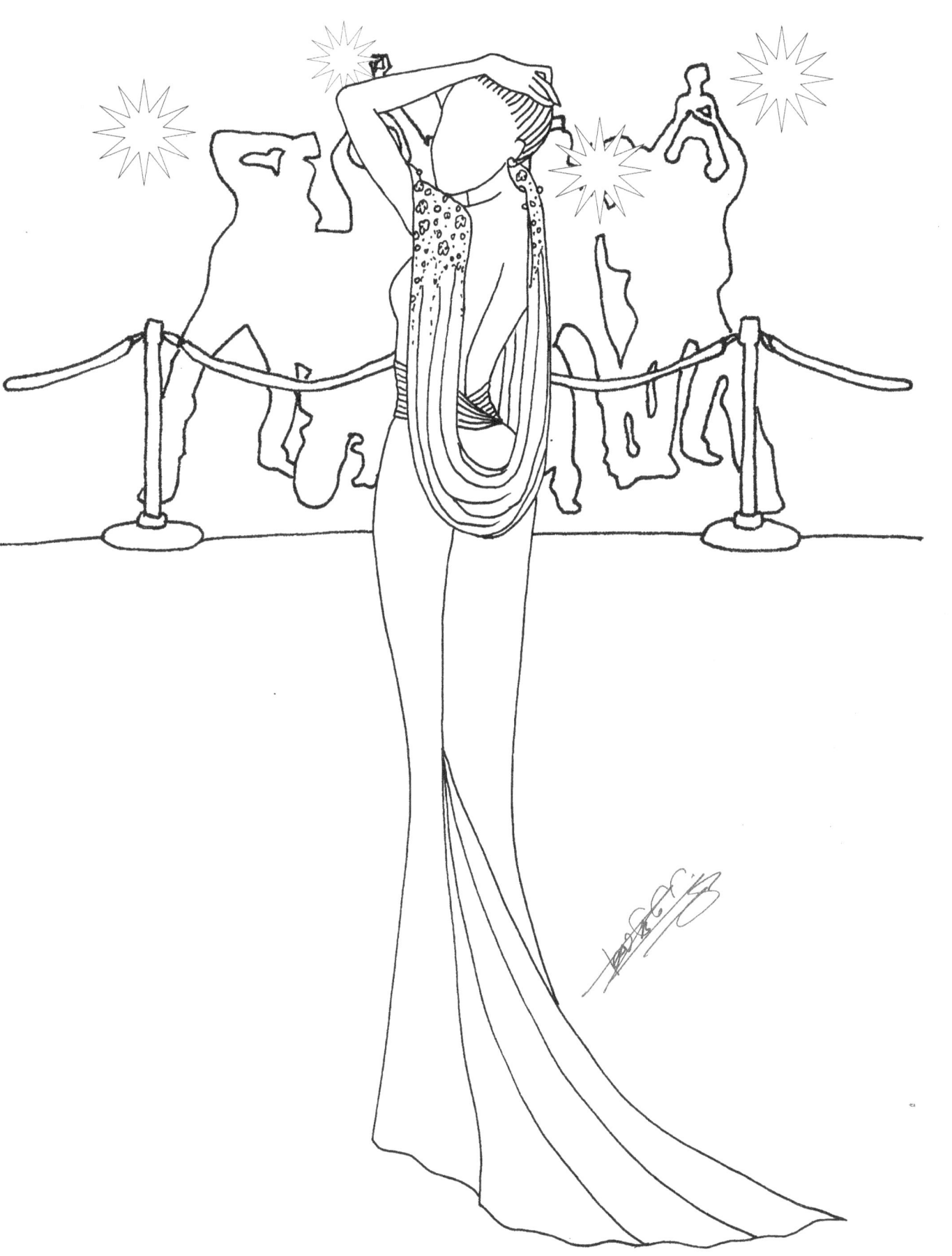

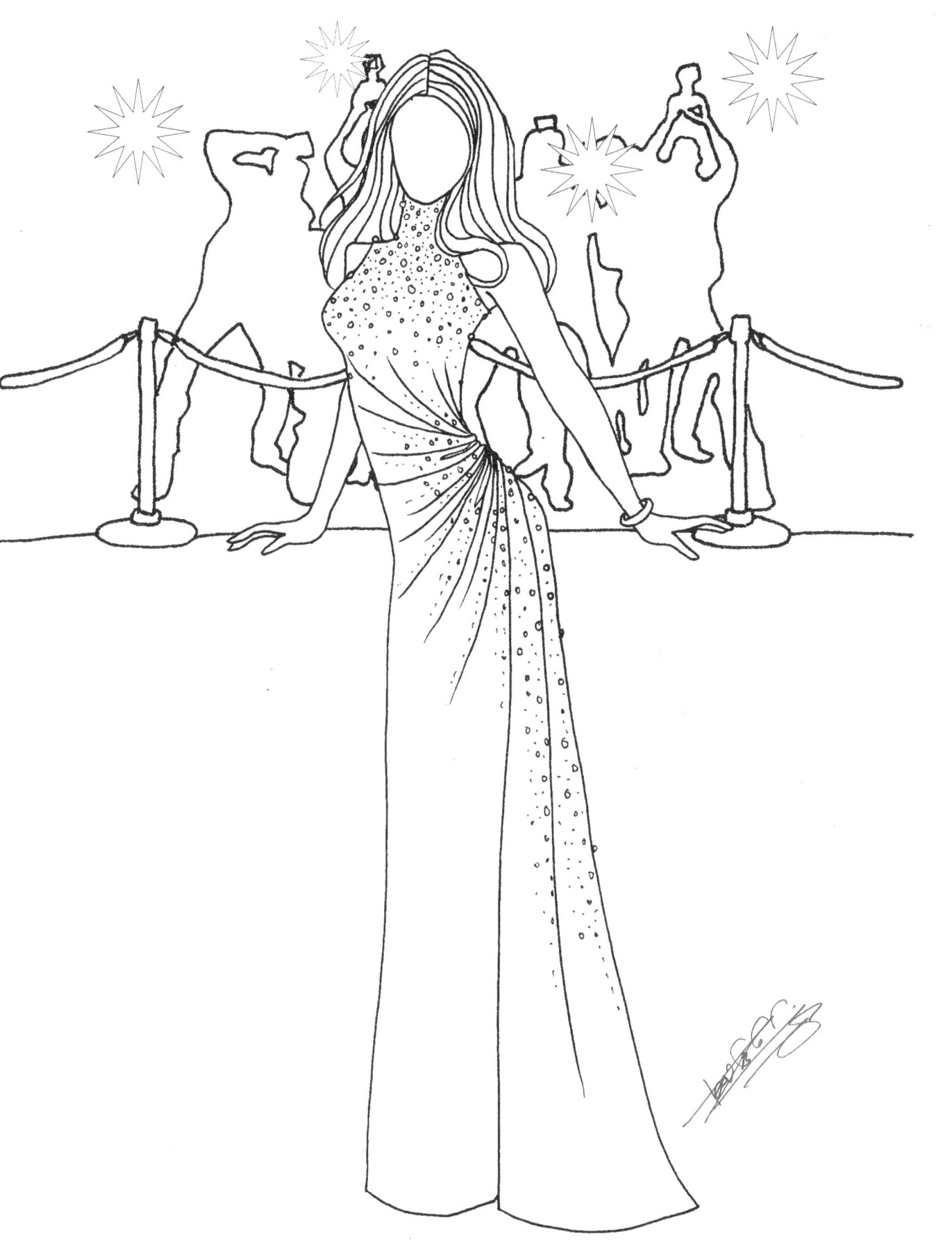

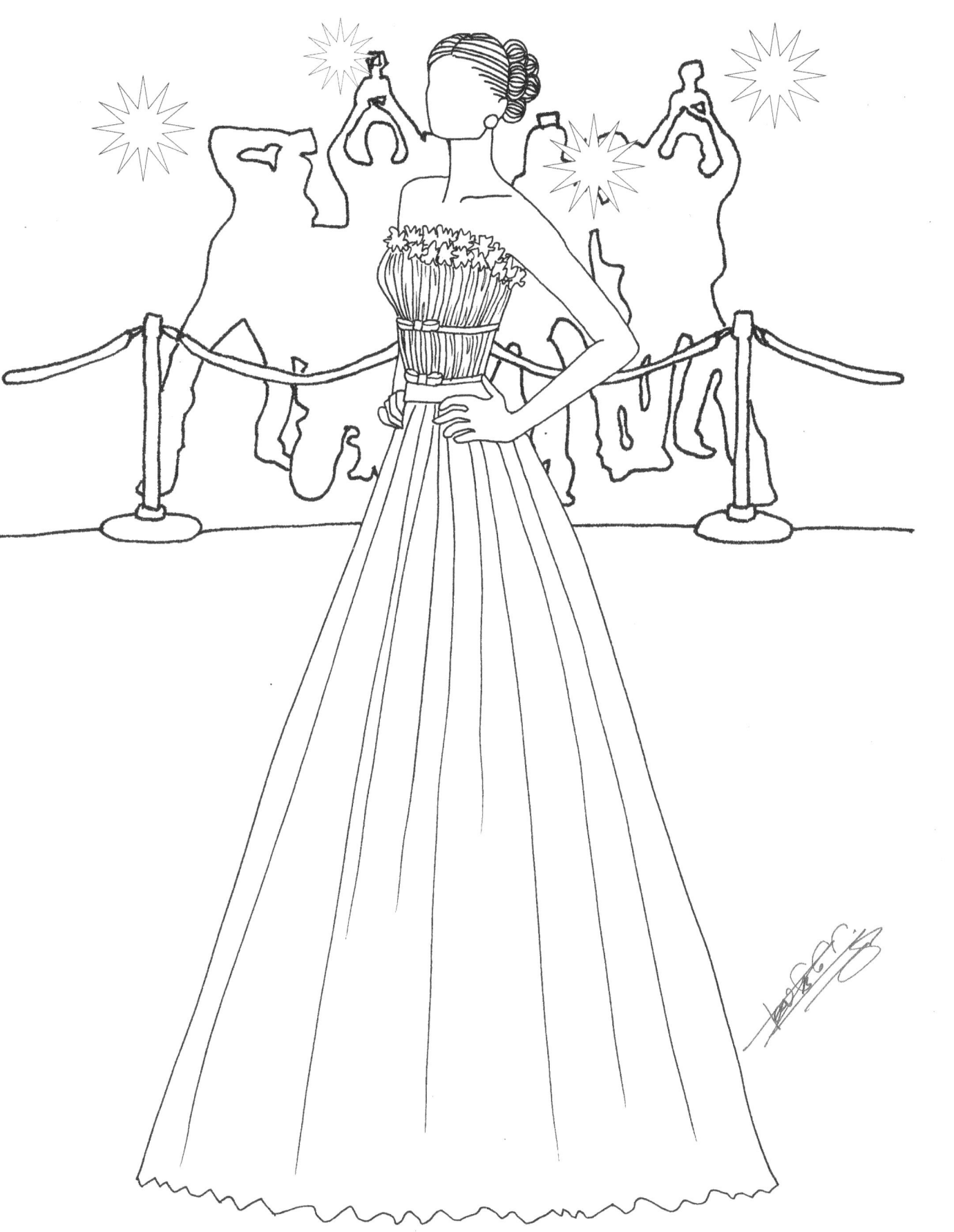

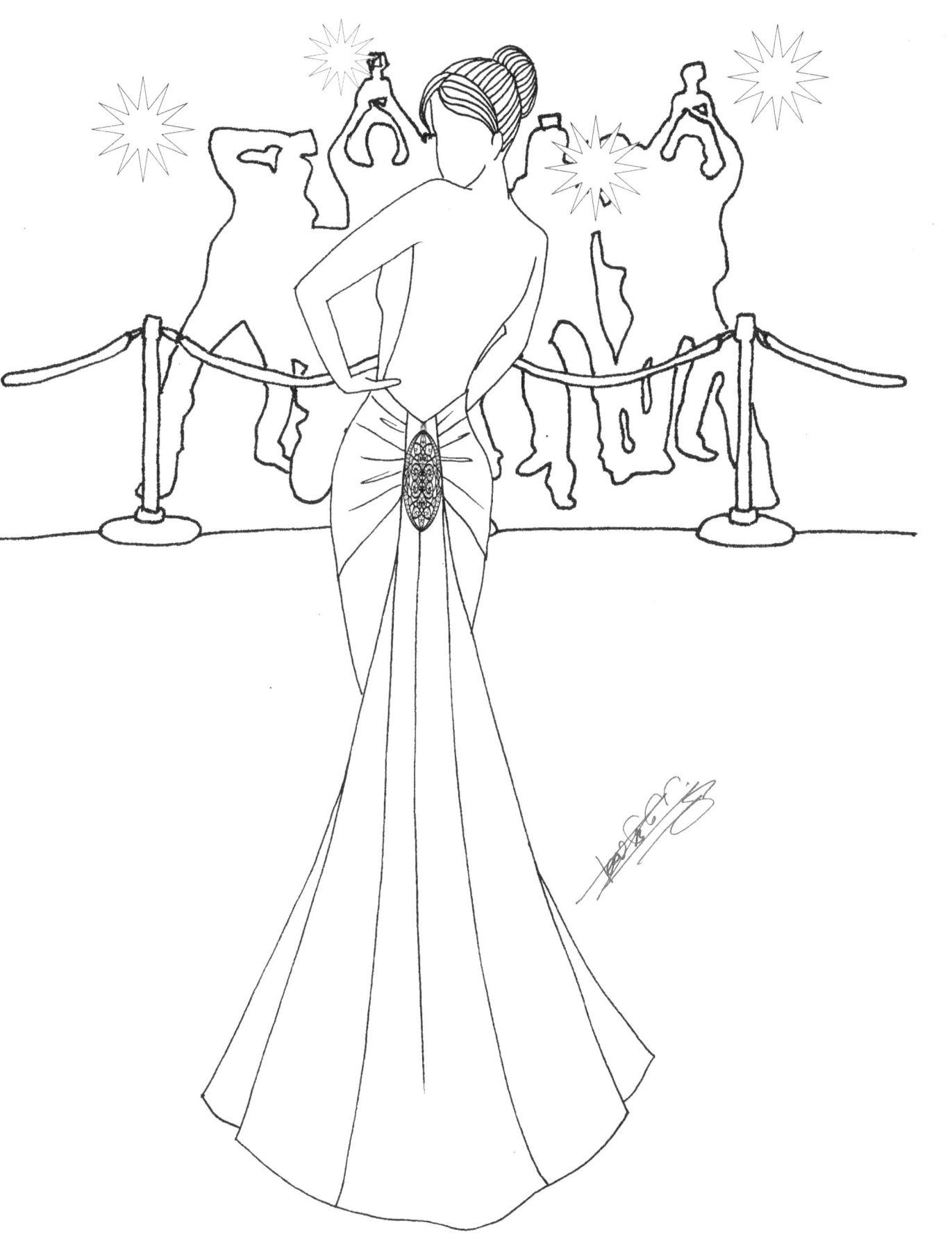

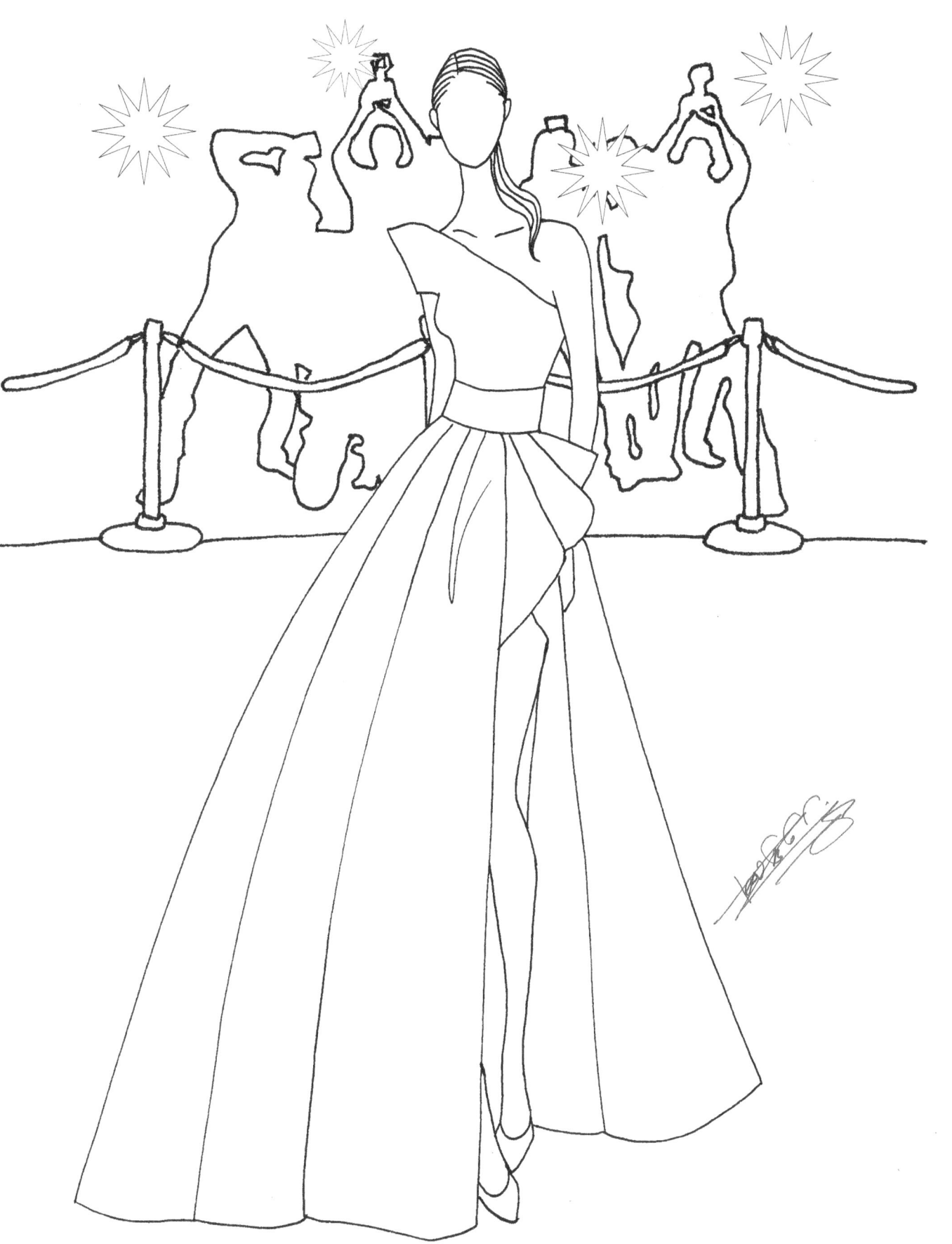

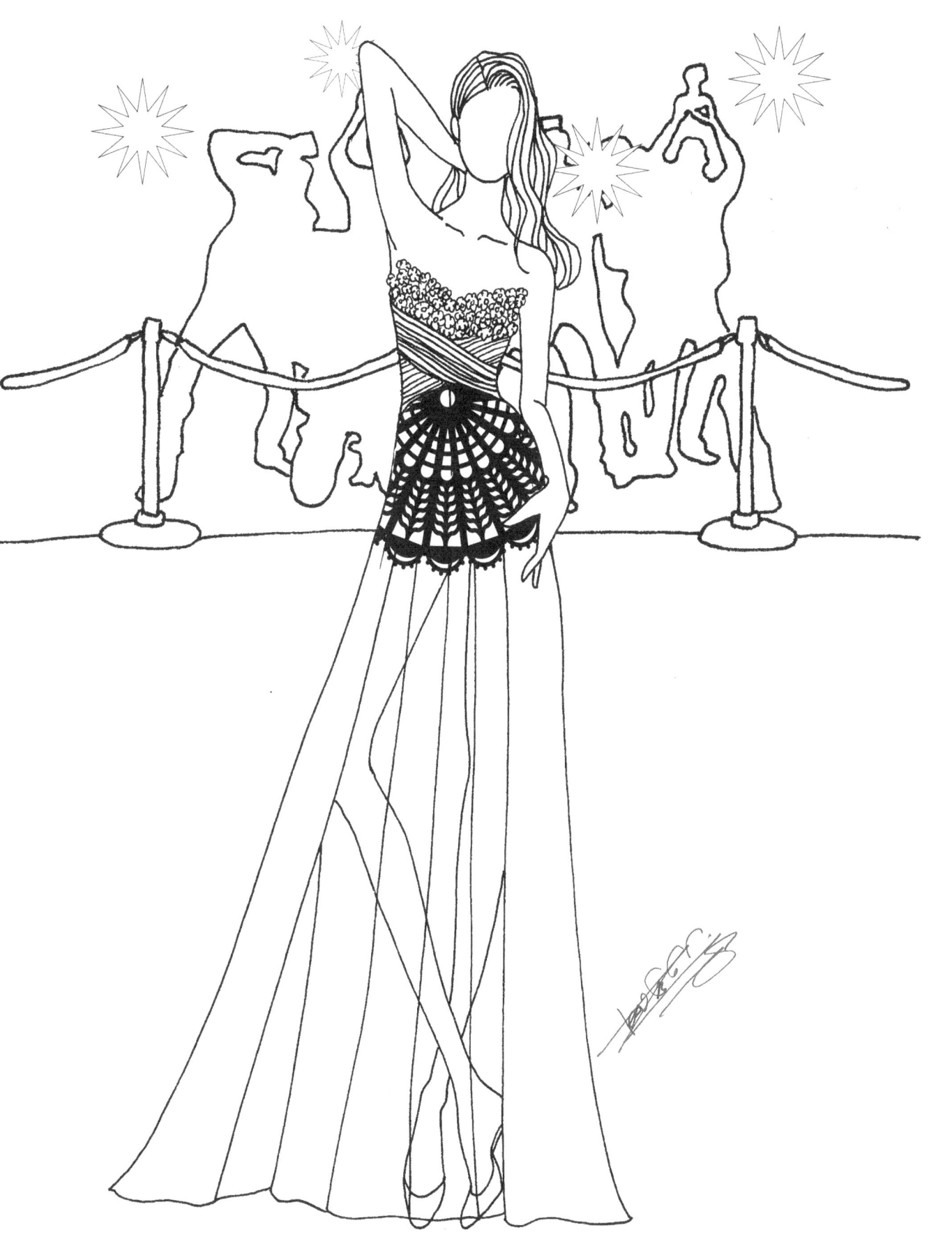

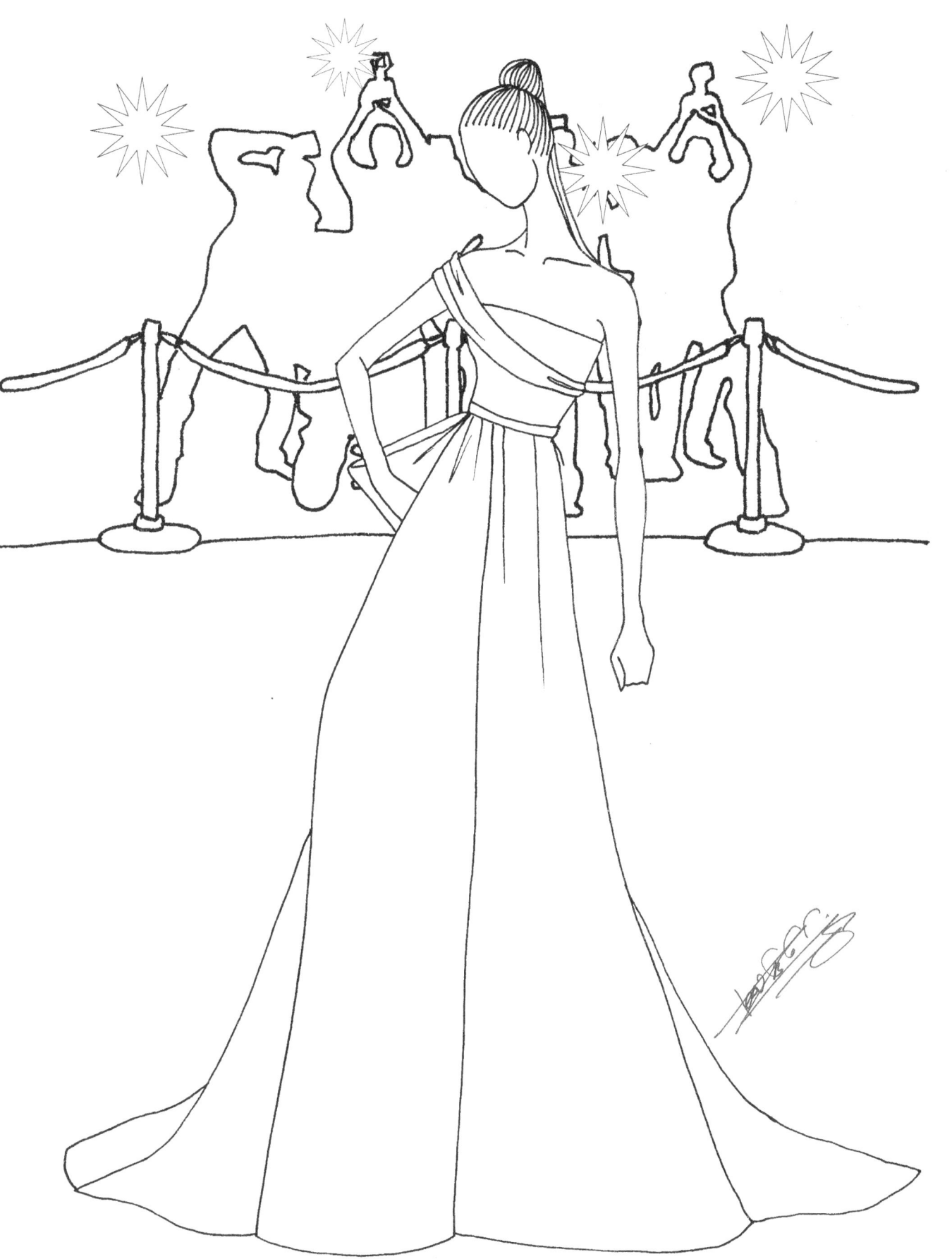

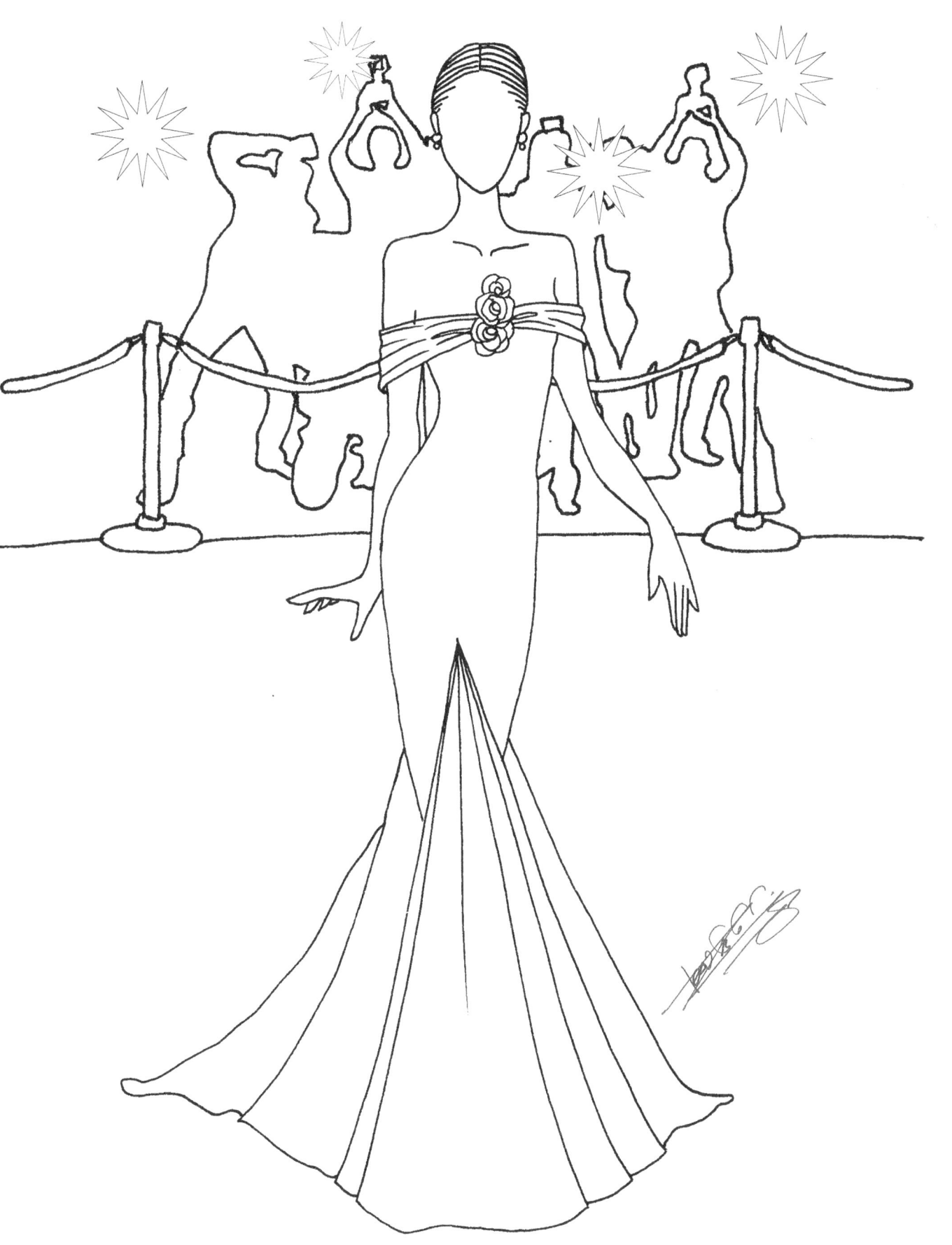

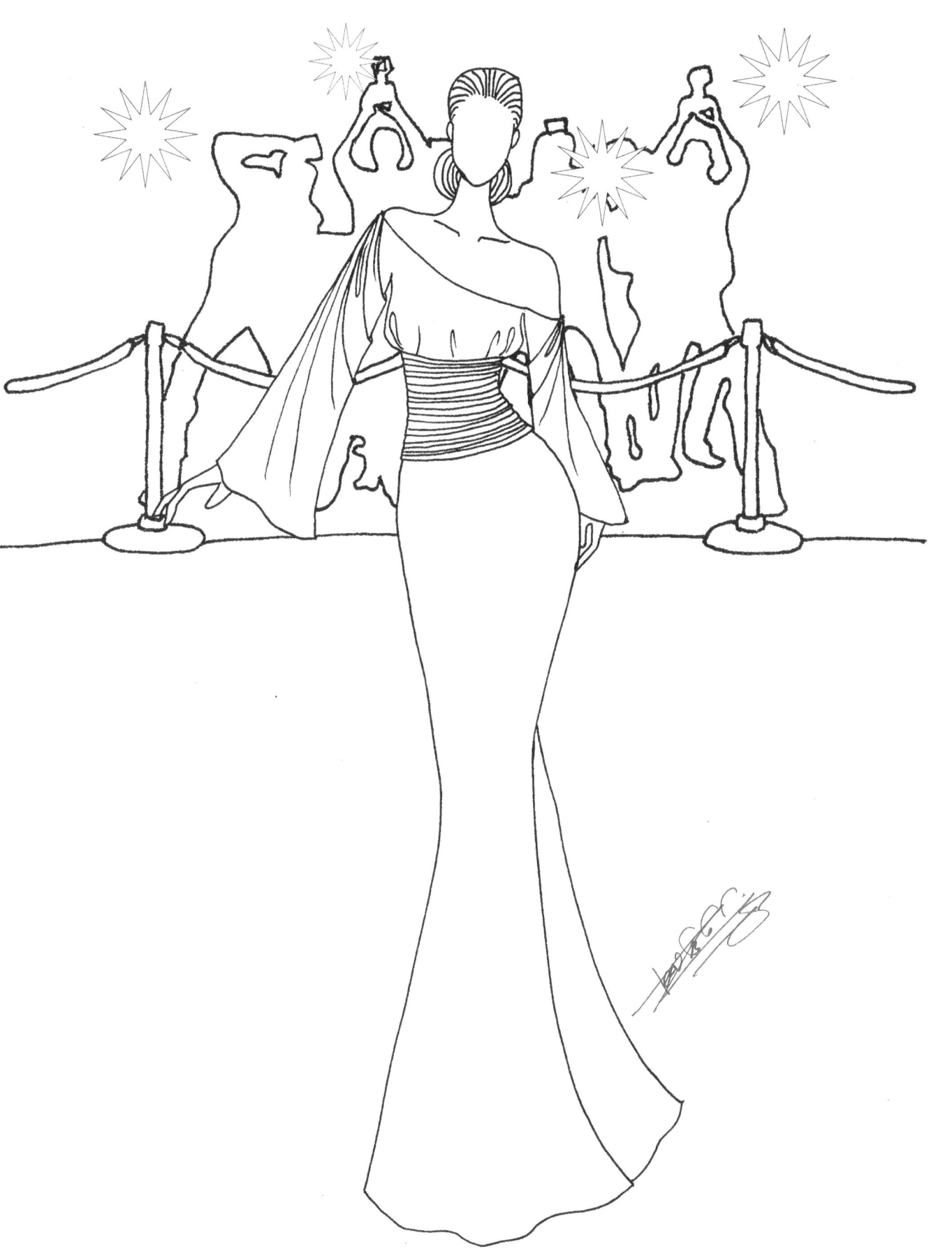

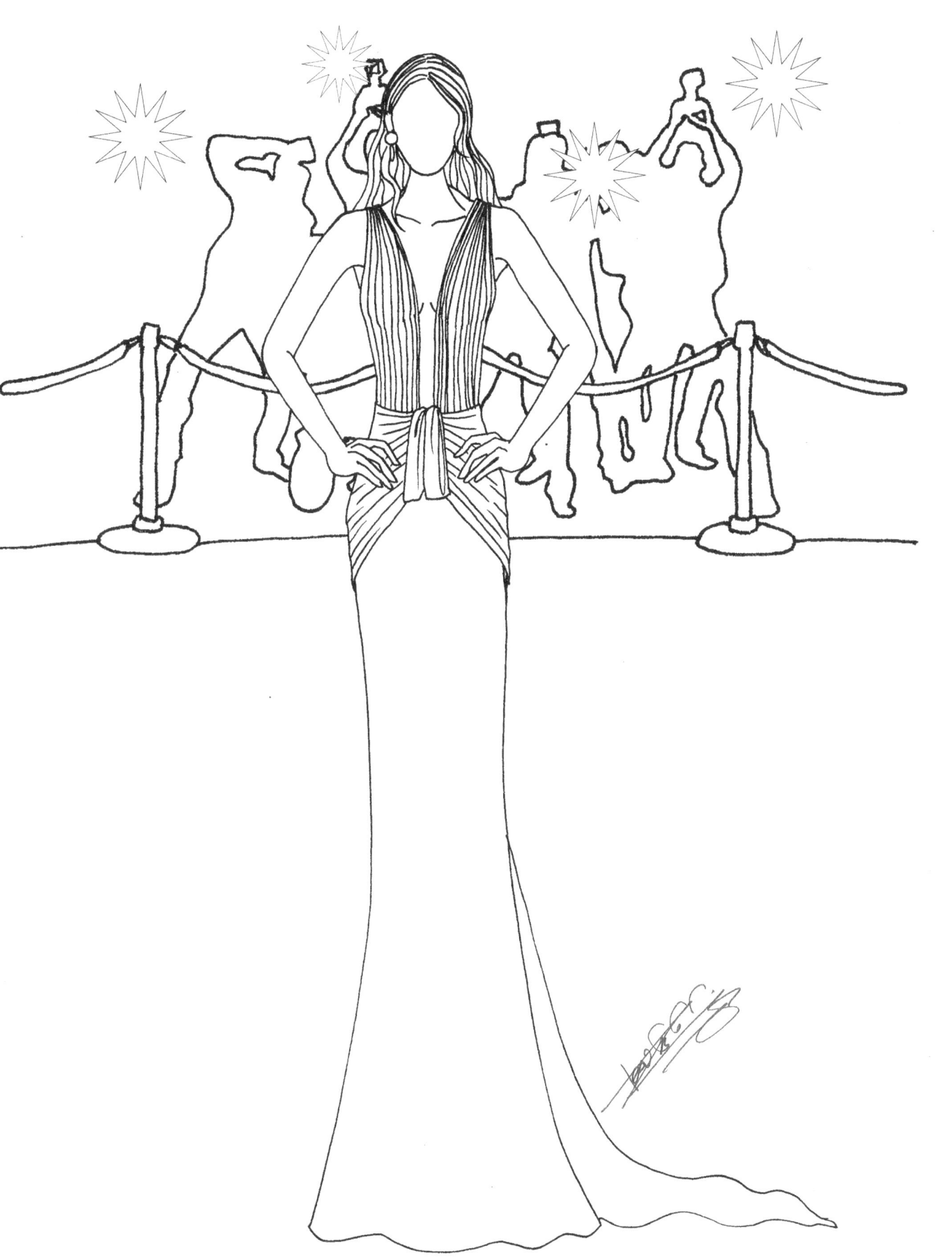

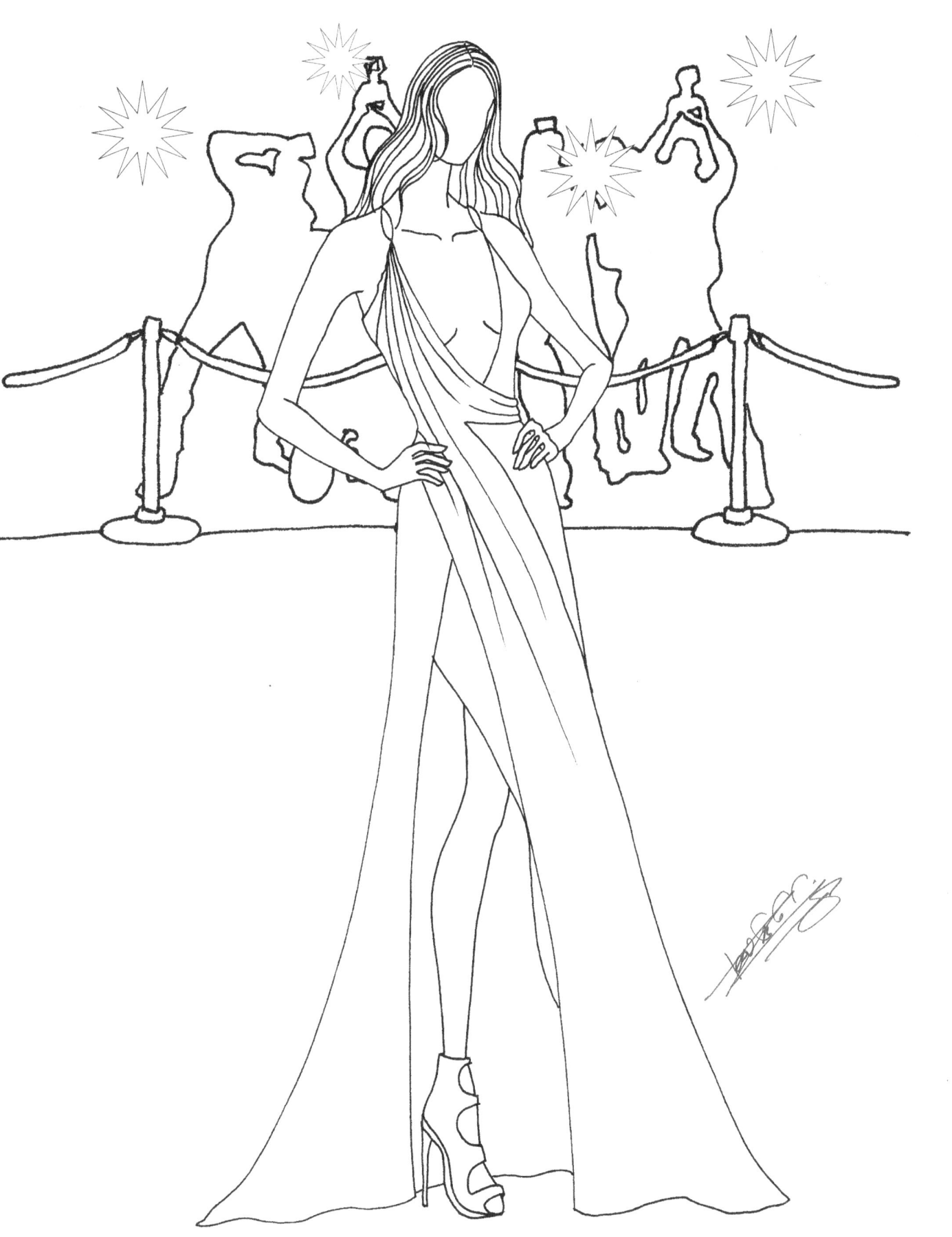

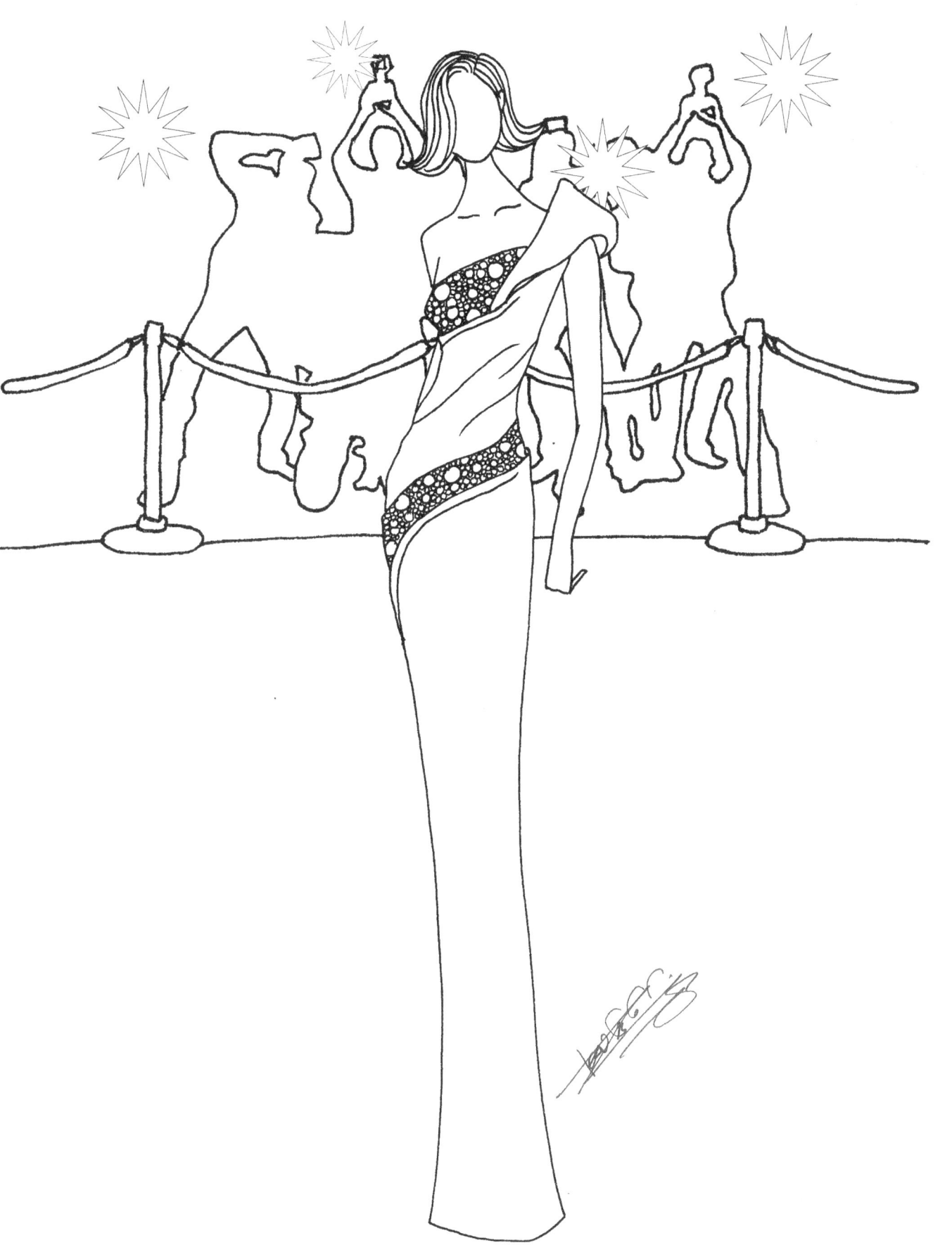

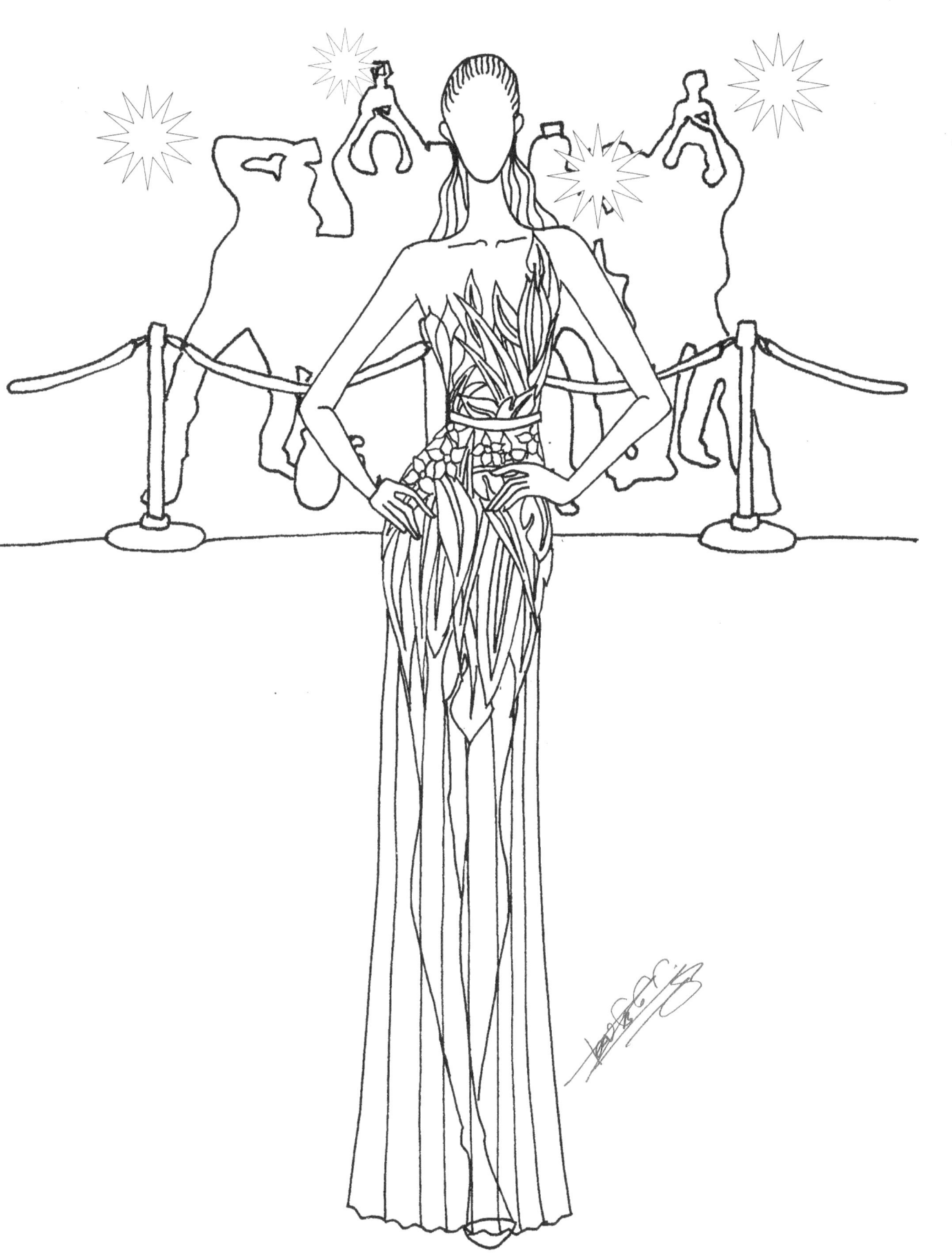

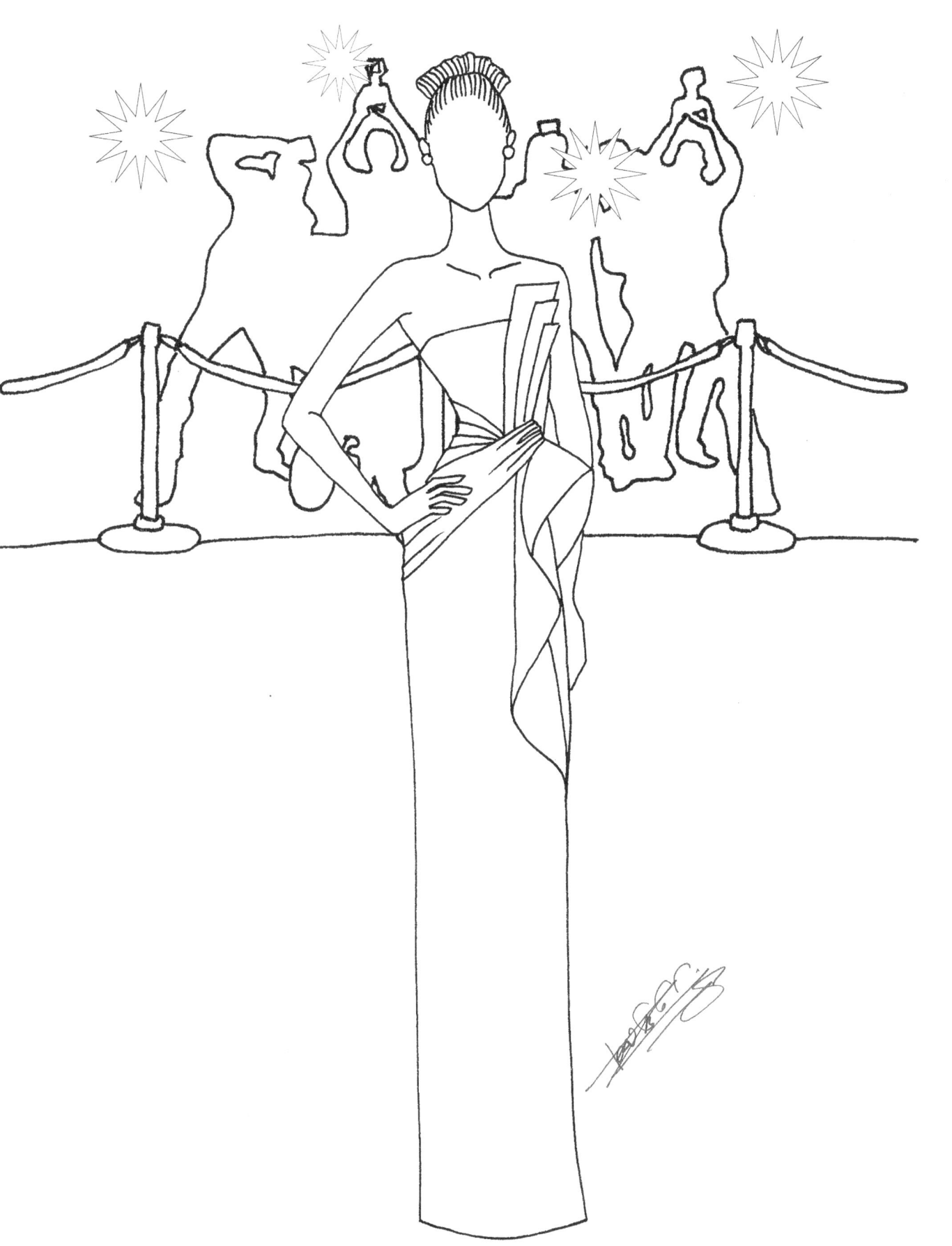

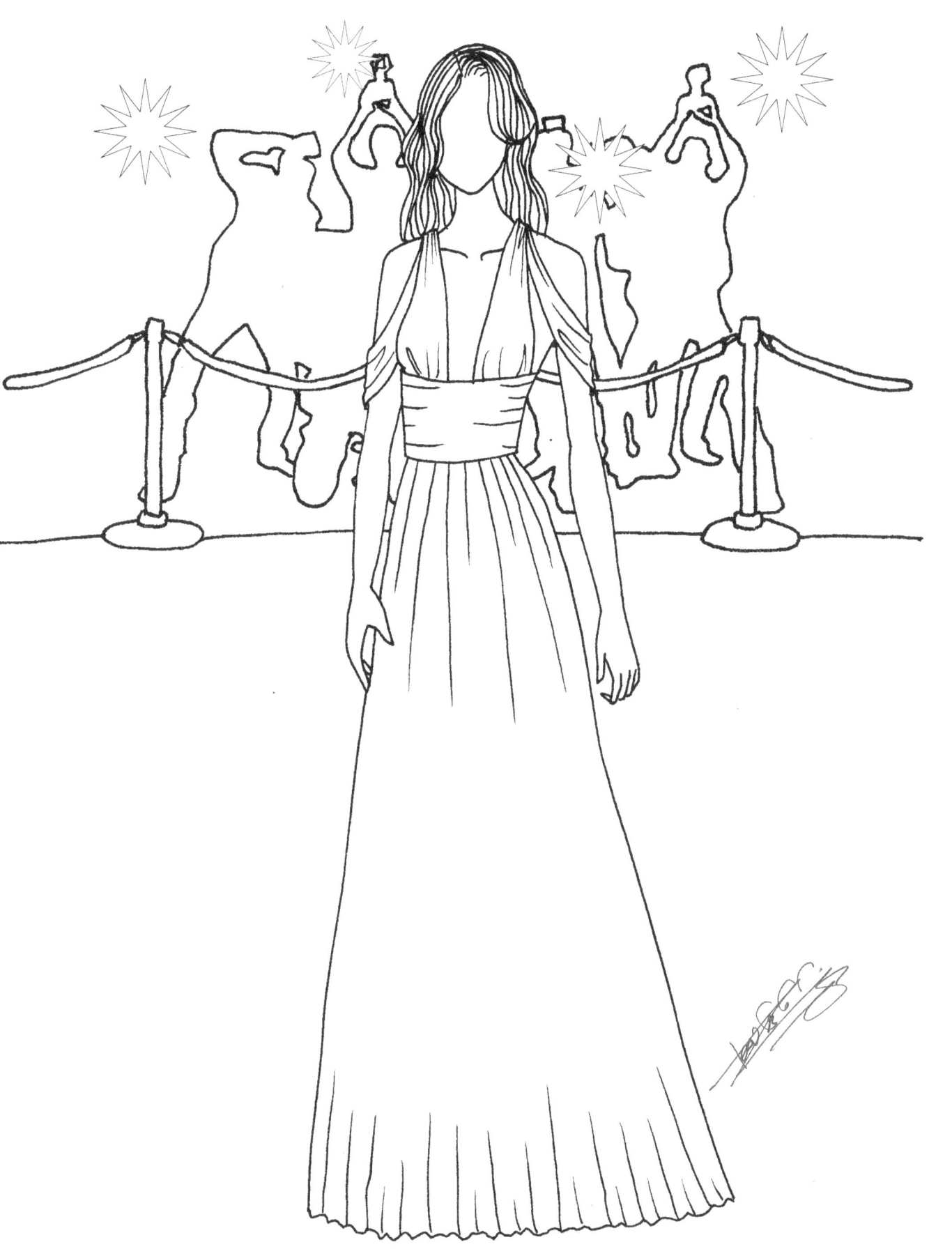

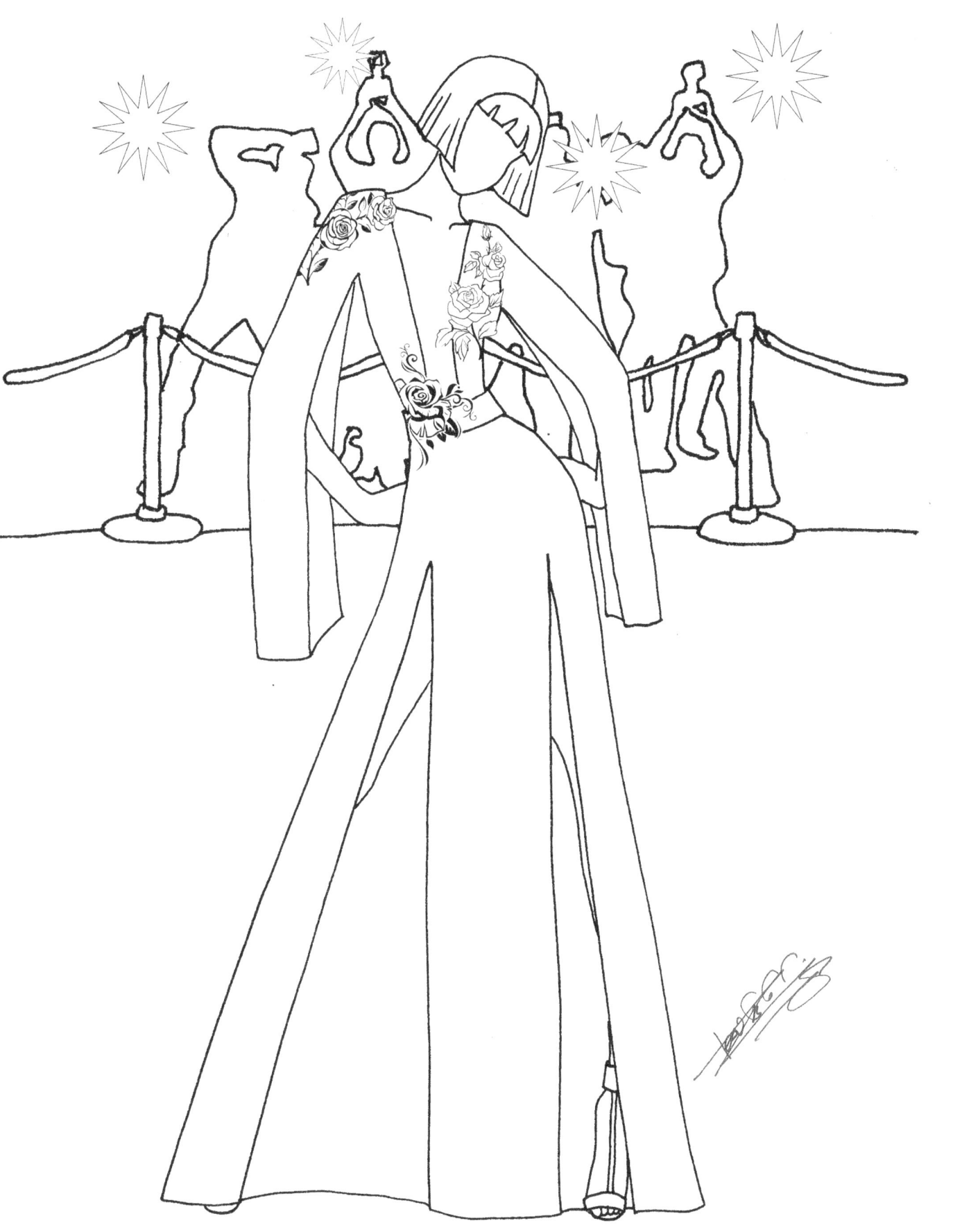

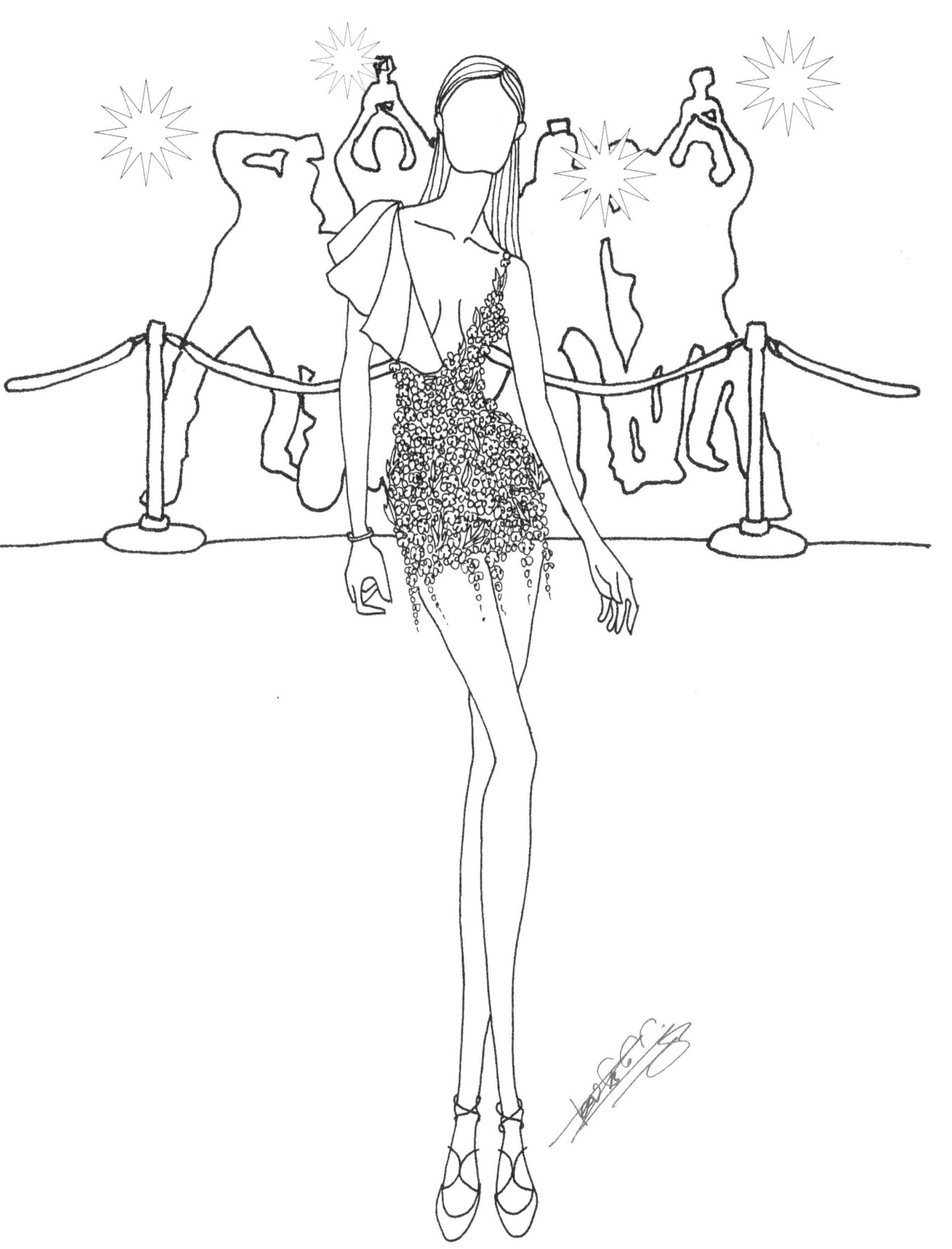

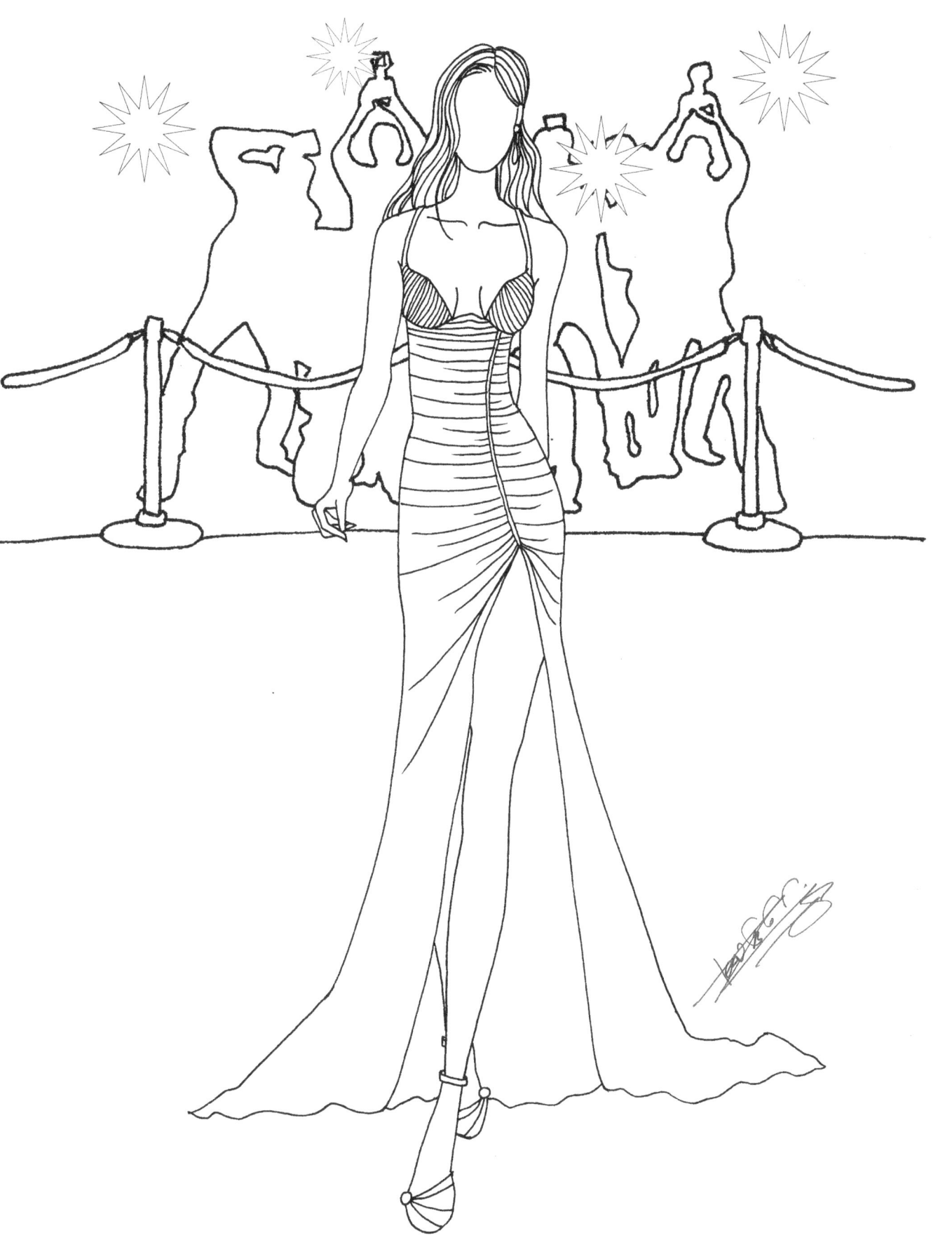

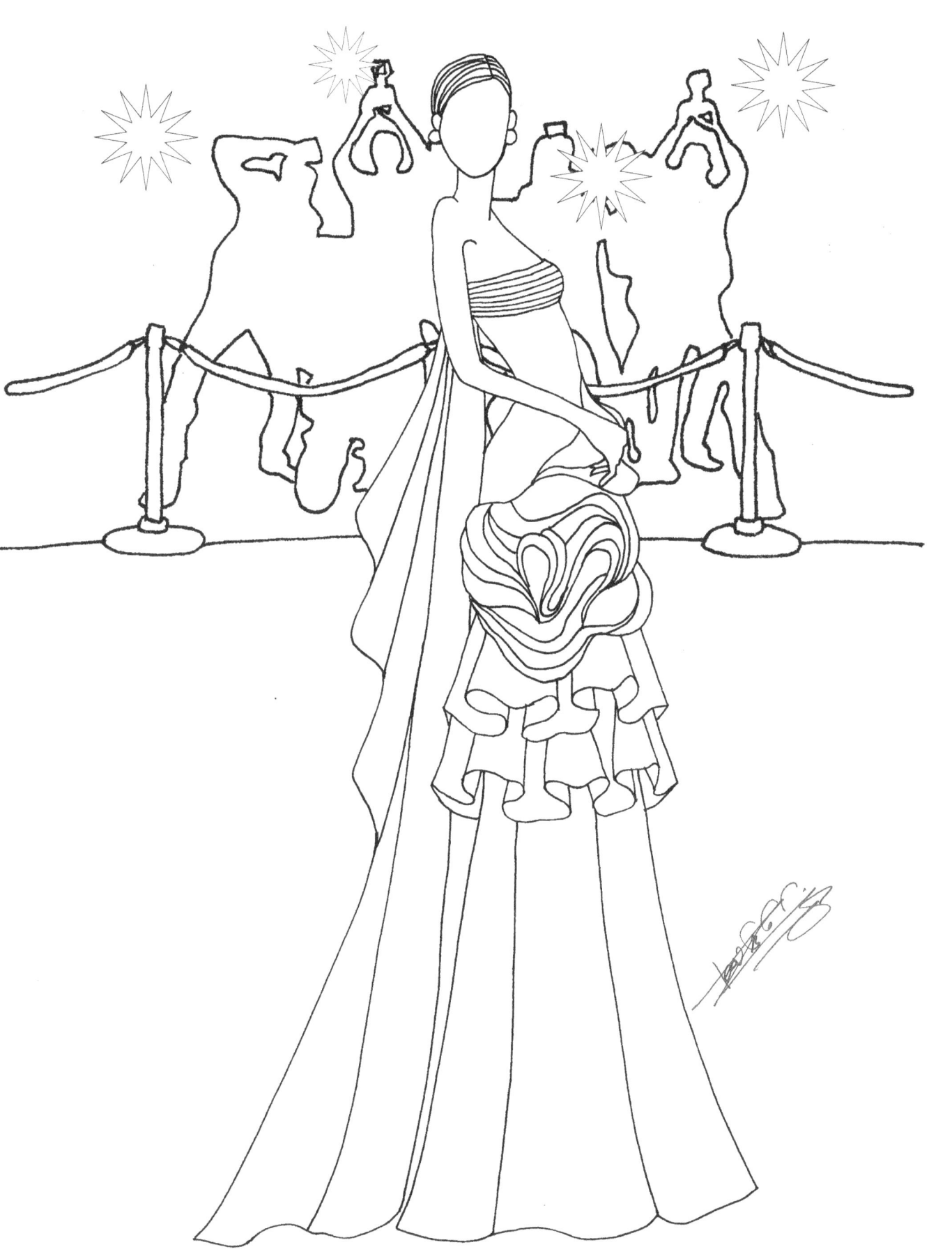

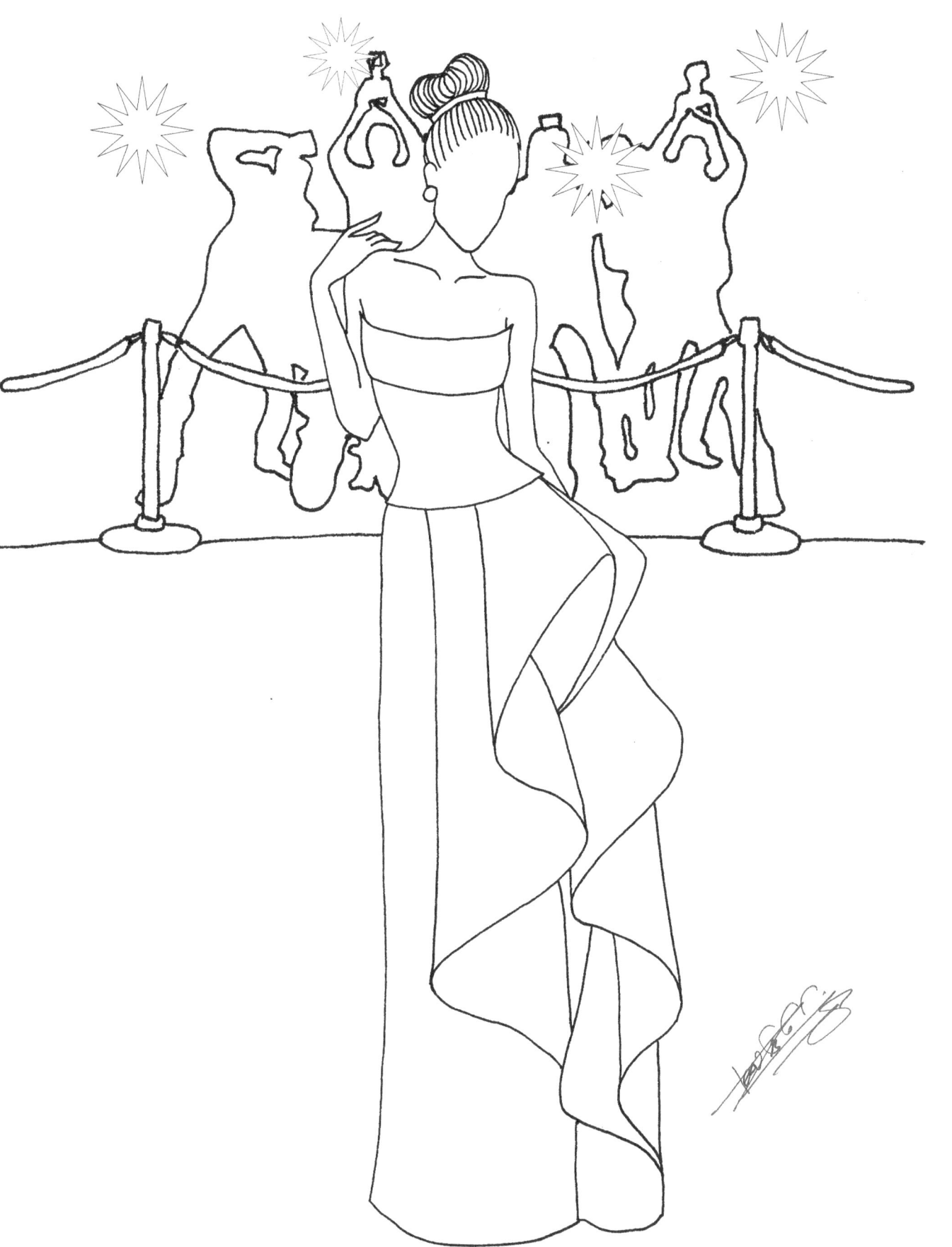

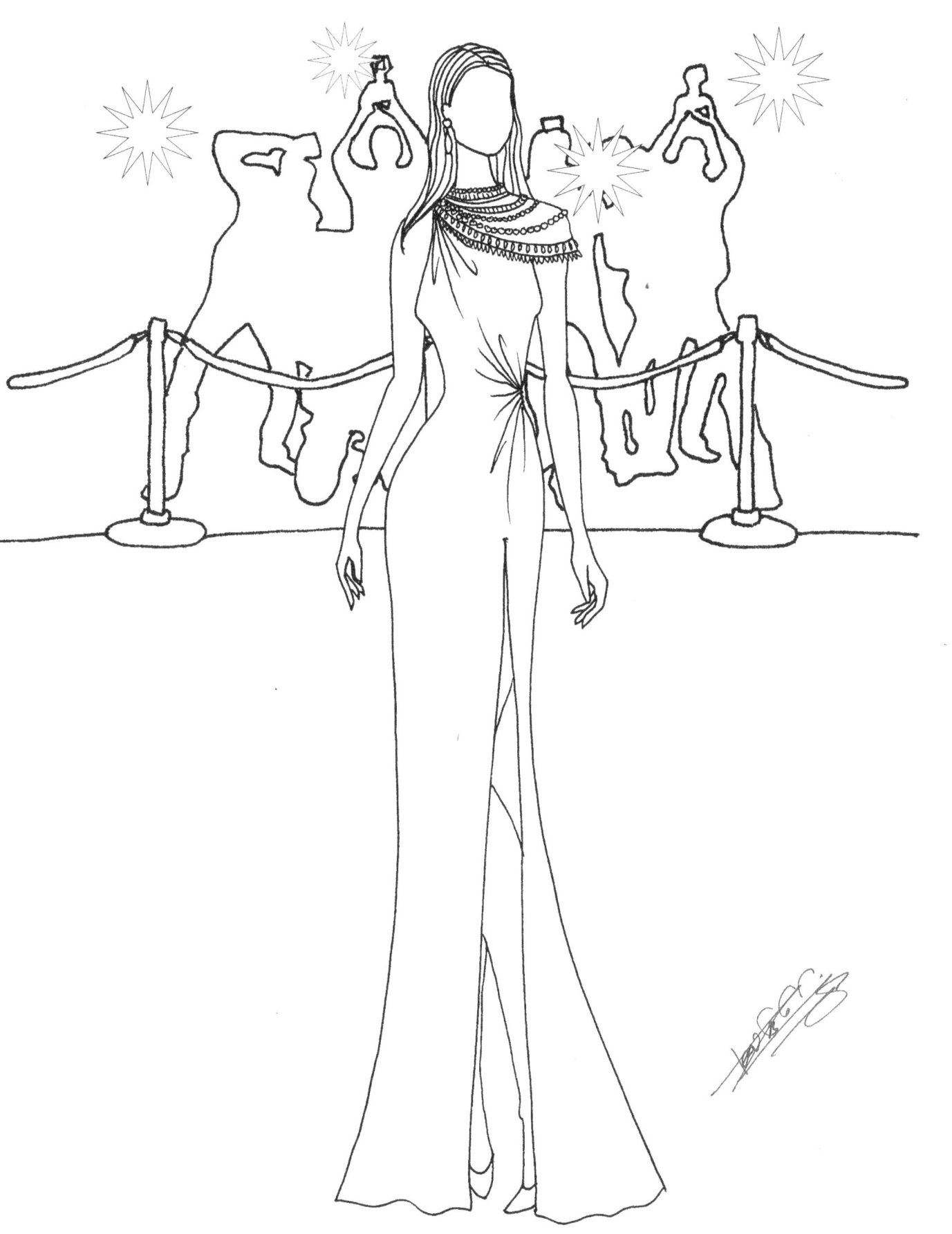

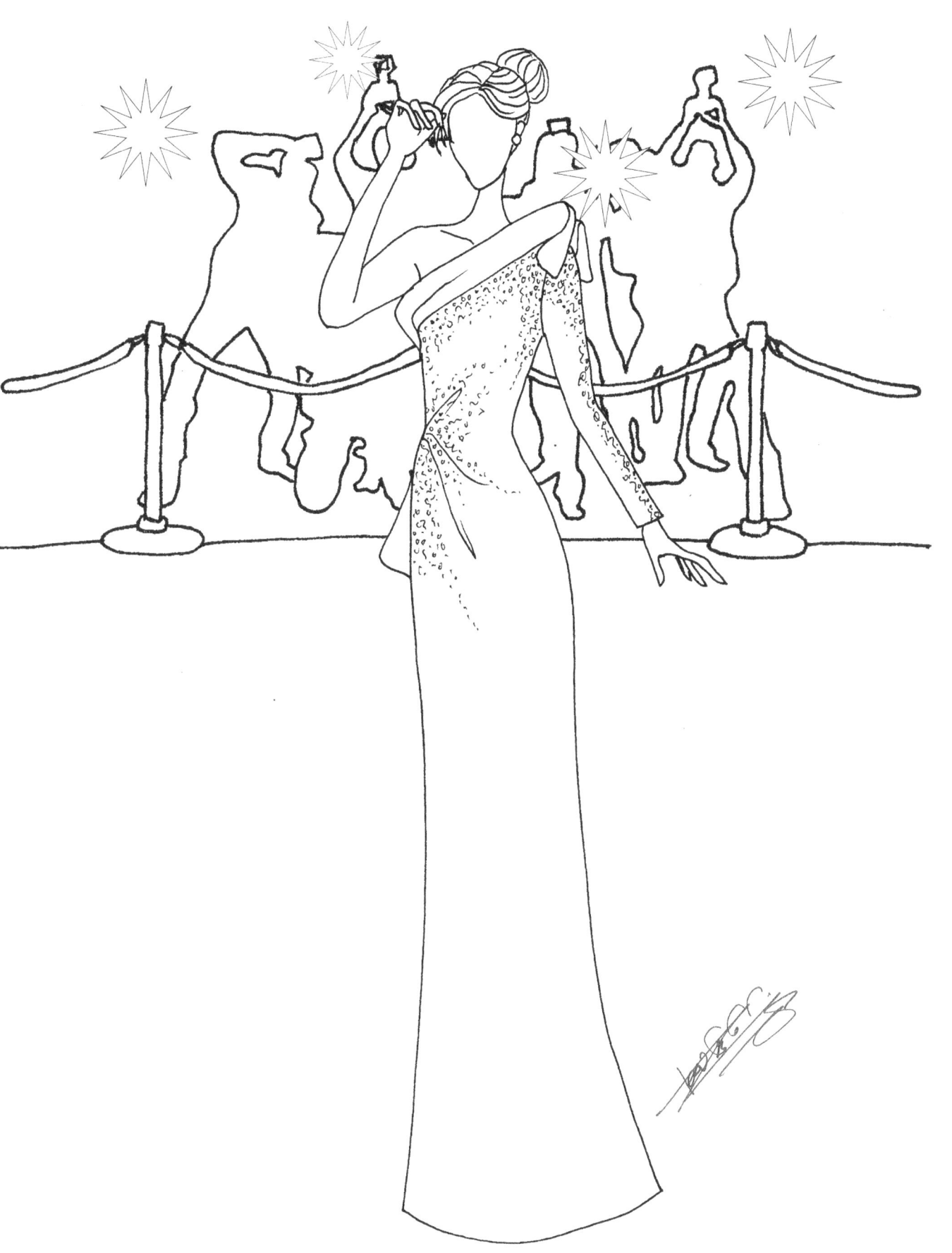

www.ingramcontent.com/pod-product-compliance
Lightning Source LLC
Chambersburg PA
CBHW081618220526
45468CB00010B/2927